SANDRA NADEGE

First Creation
A Collection of Poems

DADYMINDS PUBLISHERS INSIDER

First published by DADYMINDS PUBLISHERS INSIDER 2025

Copyright © 2025 by Sandra Nadege

All rights reserved. No part of this publication may be reproduced, stored or transmitted in any form or by any means, electronic, mechanical, photocopying, recording, scanning, or otherwise without written permission from the publisher. It is illegal to copy this book, post it to a website, or distribute it by any other means without permission.

This novel is entirely a work of fiction. The names, characters and incidents portrayed in it are the work of the author's imagination. Any resemblance to actual persons, living or dead, events or localities is entirely coincidental.

Sandra Nadege asserts the moral right to be identified as the author of this work.

Sandra Nadege has no responsibility for the persistence or accuracy of URLs for external or third-party Internet Websites referred to in this publication and does not guarantee that any content on such Websites is, or will remain, accurate or appropriate.

Learn more about the DADYMINDS Company: https://www.dadyminds.org

The Publisher: DPI (DADYMINDS PUBLISHERS INSIDER) is the TM Department in charge of book publishing and author services at DADYMINDS HOLDINGS LLC.

Email: info.dadymindsltd@gmail.com

WhatsApp: +250 (781) 355-361/+1 (307) 323-4616

Mail: 1007 North Orange Street, 4th Floor Suite #2987, Wilmington, Delaware, United States

First edition

ISBN: 979-8-3492-1991-7

Editing by Anath Lee Wales

This book was professionally typeset on Reedsy. Find out more at reedsy.com

When I am gone, tell my beloved ones to look in my poems; deep in the words, they will find my soul.

SANDRA NADEGE

Contents

Prologue   1

I   PATRIOTISM

THE STORY OF AFRICA   5
AFRICAN CHILD   11
NEED FOR NOVELTY   14

II   MATTERS OF HEARTS

MODERN YOU   21
BRING A ROSE   25
KISS YOU GOODBYE   31
FRIENDSHIP   36

III   LOVE, LIFE AND LIES

YOUR LOVE REMINDS ME…   41
I DON'T REMEMBER WHEN…   43
SLAP OF REALITY   45
THE MONSTER   47
SAVE ME   49
LOST AND NEVER FOUND   54
INFINITE LOOP   57

IV   PASSION AND SELF-LOVE

ANOTHER HEART	63
FOUNTAIN OF ECSTASY	65
FALL IN LOVE WITH POETRY	68
POET IN A WARRIOR	70
FIRST CREATION	72
Epilogue	74
Afterword	75
About the Author	77

Prologue

Poetry transcends mere ink on paper, the profound echo of a soul yearning to connect, the rhythmic pulse of deep-seated emotions aching to be heard. In "First Creation," we encounter not just a collection of poems but a raw, heartfelt outpouring from a young poetess—her innermost reflections on the tangled web of life, the sweetness and sorrow of love, and the vibrant world that envelops her. Each verse is a delicate whisper of truth, inviting readers to immerse themselves in its depths; each line serves as a luminous window into the unspoken emotions that stir within, revealing fears, dreams, and the quiet joys that make her heart beat fervently. This anthology is a journey through the labyrinth of feelings that connect us all, showcasing the power of vulnerability and the beauty of self-expression.

Within these pages, you will discover a tapestry of words intricately woven with the profound love of a motherland—Africa, a majestic land steeped in resilience and breathtaking beauty. Some poems spring forth with the fiery warmth of newfound passion, radiating joy and hope, while others resonate with the deep ache of heartbreak, reflecting the pain that often shadows our journeys. Each piece carries whispers of the universe's vast mysteries, inviting contemplation on life's unpredictable paths and the rollercoaster of emotions we navigate. Dive into the embrace of self-love, where we seek to accept and celebrate our true selves in all our complexities. This collection serves as a heartfelt invitation to explore life's raw, unfiltered realities and feel the rhythm of untamed emotions that intimately connect us.

Let the words wrap around you like a warm hug, stirring memories and feelings long forgotten, urging you to explore the depths of your heart and soul.

First Creation transcends mere words; it delves into the raw honesty of our deepest emotions. These are not just poems; they are whispers of the heart, capturing truths you may have felt but never dared to voice. They embody the unarticulated, those feelings that linger in the shadows, now illuminated for you. Allow them to resonate within you, to stir your spirit—embark on this profound journey through the landscapes of love, the ache of loss, and the soul's most profound yearnings.

I

PATRIOTISM

Love of our land and people

THE STORY OF AFRICA

***

Blood moon glows in the silent night,
Pots simmer low, fire burning bright.
No necks craning, no forks in sight,
Just hands and hearts, holding tight.

**

No silverware clinking, no need for gold,
Only souls linking, stories told.
Under the sky, so deep, so red,
We feast on love, on words unsaid.

***

Their music pounds, fierce and wild,
Not slow, not soft, not meek or mild.
No waltzing steps, no graceful glide,
Just pulsing beats and hearts open wide.

**

Sweating bodies, burning skin,
Palms that sting, yet souls draw in.

Nevertheless, through heat and song,
Hearts are joining, fierce and strong.

***

There's love, no fear, no walls to tear,
Clothes are worn, but hearts are bare.
Sheep are sheared, their wool so pure,
Meat gets shared, and spirits endure.

**

Hope is strong, it cannot break,
Together, they rise for unity's sake.
No shattered dreams, no dark despair,
Just a world of love, a bond to share.

***

The skins are dark, not coloured bright,
Easy breaths are scarce in the night.
When spirits rise, the air grows thick,
Everybody feels the pull, the trick.

**

Grudges fade like shadows tall,
Mauled by the wind, broken, small.
In the heat of the ritual, hearts are laid,
Seeking peace in the light and the shade.

***

The continent is dark, deep as the night,
Rough and rugged, yet full of light.
Lively, vibrant, with a pulse so strong,
A spirit that's endured, unwavering all along.

**

Yet, sadly, it goes unnoticed, unseen,
Its strength is hidden behind the veil of routine.
But in its heart, the fire will burn,
For the world will one day, finally, return.

***

It's home, where I'm never alone,
The troubles fade, and the weight is gone.
Whenever Mama calls me to eat some,
I know, despite the world, this place is not gruesome.

**

Here, love is woven in every thread,
In every meal, in every word said.
For in this space, I feel alive,
In the warmth of home, I thrive.

***

It is not perfect, yet it's compact,
A land of strength, though the orders lacked.
Leaders' voices, discordant and loud,
Guiding battles through a stormy cloud.

**

They watched as their lands were taken away,
As victories turned to dust and grey.
But still, the spirit of the people stands,
Holding on to dreams with steady hands.

***

On the battlefields, spears were killing,
Guns were firing, hearts unwilling.

And love, once strong, was slipping away,
As children wept, refusing to lie.

**

With all that blood spilling on the ground,
Silent cries were the only sound.
In the chaos, hope seemed far,
Yet still, some hearts wished on a star.

***

The place was a jungle, wild and free,
The people knew neither of Christmas nor the tree.
The whites began to mingle, to weave their spell,
Tossing Christendom like a jingle bell.

**

In catching it, they lost their way,
Their freedom is fading, day by day.
To the white man, they gave their trust,
But in the end, the cost was just.

***

Their ways were not clean, far from pure,
They said they shouldn't be seen, to endure.
Taught the mothers to be lean,
While the children grew cold, sharp, and mean.

**

They broke the bonds, they stole the light,
Shrouding the land in endless nights.
But through the pain, the hearts still yearned,
For a brighter day, for a world to be returned.

***

They had technology in their chronology,
Biology and tautology are all part of their ideology.
Ophthalmology and phonology, they claimed as their own,
They thought they had invented it, yet the seeds were already sown.

**

But they got it all inverted, the truth lost in the spin,
For what they called progress was a cycle to begin.
In their hands, the tools of the past,
Yet they failed to see the wisdom that would last.

***

After they came, our lives were changed,
The world we knew was rearranged.
We entered a game, not for fame,
But to light a flame, to end the shame.

**

A spark of hope for our land to rise,
A dream that could not be disguised.
Through struggle, we found our way,
To bring a brighter, better day.

***

Yes, we dropped the witches,
And took on the switches.
We faced the wickedest,
Tackled the wildest,

**

But still, in our hearts, we strive,
To thrive, to feel alive.

Chasing riches, chasing dreams,
Hoping to find the light that gleams.

***

What's wrong with a few flaws?
As long as we stay out of the devil's claws?
We won't crawl, not anymore,
We've taken blows, we've felt the war.

**

But still, we rise, we stand so tall,
Through every storm, we never fall.
We've survived before, through loss and pain,
And we will rise, over and over again.

***

We won't beg a son of man,
No one would hear or understand.
We will learn, we will strive,
Keep the fire in us alive.

**

Welfare is distant, the road is long,
But we are fierce; we are strong.
Through the struggle, come what may,
It'll all be alright one day.

(The journey might seem so long, but don't stop, take a break, remember that you're brave, and then continue)

AFRICAN CHILD

***

Oh, African child, so bold, so bright,
Born from struggle, forged in light.
My shoulder is here; lean if you must,
But never let go of hope and trust.

**

Cry if you must, let the pain flow,
Yet smile, for strength is what you show.
Through every trial, through every spell,
Your heart's light will break it well.

***

My ears will listen, soft and wide,
To the sorrow, you hold inside.
But tell me, love, what can I do,
To ease the pain and walk with you?

**

Shall I lift you when you fall?
Stand beside you, proud and tall?

Or simply hold your hand so tight,
And guide you gently to the light?

***

Come, fall into my open arms,
Let me shield you from life's harm.
Come, tell me of your hopes and dreams,
Though the world is not as kind as it seems.

**

Yes, struggle lingers, fierce and cold,
Hunger, death, and war take hold.
But you don't have to stand alone,
Together, we can build a home.

***

But there's beauty in this world, you see,
In the rivers, the sky, the tallest tree.
The sun still rises, the flowers bloom,
Hope will shine through even the gloom.

**

Be resilient, stand tall, and fight,
Hold on to dreams with all your might.
Oh, African child, remember this—
Even the most extended night ends in bliss.

***

Strive for what you hold so dear,
Let nothing shake your heart with fear.
Keep the fire burning bright,
Through every storm, through the darkest night.

**

One day soon, the dawn will rise,
With golden hope in endless skies.
And we will stand, so proud, so free,
Rejoicing together in victory.

NEED FOR NOVELTY

***

Our place is adorned with fine horizons,
Where the sun wakes in golden prisms.
It climbs high to kiss the sky,
Then sinks behind mountains, waving goodbye.

**

The rivers hum, the valleys sigh,
The wind whispers as clouds drift by.
A land so rich, so bold, so vast,
Where dreams and nature walk side by side.

***

In season, when rain is drizzling,
Its melody is soft, almost mesmerizing.
So tranquil, yet intensely thrilling,
A rhythm of life is so fulfilling.

**

Each drop whispers a promise,
Of fields of green and harvests of gold.

The earth drinks deep, the rivers rise,
As nature blooms beneath grey skies.

***

Despite it all, we remember well,
How our elders in humble huts did dwell.
The sight of hungry children aches,
A pain that no heart quickly shakes.

**

But let us not flee, nor turn away,
From the soil where our roots still lay.
Instead, let's rise, let's stand upright,
And for our land, let's fiercely fight.

***

Over the years, the faces tell,
A story of sorrow, a tale of hell.
So grim, so worn, so filled with pain,
As if they'll never smile again.

**

But we, the young, must change the tide,
With hope and fire burning inside.
Let's rise, let's build, let's dream so deep,
And lock a bright future in our grip.

***

We are tired of being seen as trash,
It's time to rise, to break the leash and dash.
Poverty grips us, but we won't stay weak,
We'll start afresh, the future we seek.

**

We'll work not just for food alone,
But for a land we can proudly own.
With sweat and will, we'll break the chain,
And build a life beyond the pain.

***

If you're wise,
Open your eyes,
This is not chasing flies,
And remember all those cries
Never earned a man a prize.

**

It's action, not despair,
That brings the change we seek to share.
Lift your head, embrace the fight,
For in your hands lies the future's light.

***

Stop hovering,
Sit and use your clever mind.
The game is not over,
We must say, "Failure, never!"

**

We face reality, we can't run forever,
We rise and fight and stand together.
With courage, strength, and hearts so bold,
We'll shape the future and break the mould.

***

Don't hide in a ditch,

Come out, stand tall, and keep watch.
Always awake, eyes wide for the catch,
We have the dignity to patch,
And pride that needs a retouch.

**

Rise from the shadows, stand in the light,
Our future is ours, within our sight.
With strength and grace, we'll reclaim our worth,
And restore the glory of our birth.

***

No more lying low,
We'll search for a safe trail to follow.
Get all folks in tow,
Take it slow, and let our spirits grow.

**

With each step, we'll pave the way,
And hopefully, in the end, we'll sway—
To the rhythm of a brighter day,
Where our hearts and dreams can stay.

***

We may feel like outcasts,
But we must build something that will last.
Maybe our dreams won't come so fast,
But let's stay silent; our voices won't rust,

**

For there will be a time, a moment so sweet,
When we'll rise and our victory greet.
With patience and strength, we'll claim our right,

And shout our triumph into the night.

***

Let's start an enlightenment,
Empower every department.
Enhance development,
As we pursue contentment,

**

We are the ones who hold the key,
To revive our land, set it free.
With vision, strength, and unity,
We'll build a future for all to see.

II

MATTERS OF HEARTS

Stories of love rejection and heart break

MODERN YOU

***

We spent our childhood.
In the same neighbourhood,
You always were in strange moods,
Like a flower that would never bloom.

**

Your silence spoke louder than words,
A mystery wrapped in gentle curves.
But beneath the quiet, I could see,
A strength waiting to set you free.

***

Honestly, I thought you were funny,
Though many found you uncanny.
I know your family wasn't one to pinch pennies,
Still, you followed your path to make more money.

**

You walked through life at your own pace,
Chasing dreams, finding your place.

Despite the odds, you stayed true,
And built a world that was all you.

***

I always stared at you in class,
A quiet mystery, a moment that would pass.
You were the class nerd, so focused, so bright,
Your eyes never strayed from the board's light.

**

Even after school, you'd disappear,
I never saw more of you, year after year.
A shadow in the hallways, you'd quietly fade,
But something about you always stayed.

***

Many called you a fool,
Said you weren't cool.
But I knew you didn't care about their looks,
You were lost in your world of books.

**

I secretly wished I could be someone you'd like,
To walk in your shoes, share in your strike.
While others judged, I saw through the veil,
And hoping for a chance where our paths might sail.

***

I always wanted you to take me dancing,
But you didn't even date,
You seemed distant, never advancing,
Yet, in my eyes, you were never second-rate.

MODERN YOU

**

You looked boring to the crowd, not to me,
A quiet soul, deep as the sea.
Now, all the girls they can't ignore,
This modern you, who they adore.

***

On prom night,
I hoped you'd ask me to be your date,
You didn't
And I lost all hope.

***

Now, you waltz back into my life,
Ten years later, full of strife.
Looking so tawny, my heart breaks once more,
As memories flood, I can't ignore them.

**

Yet you claim you've always loved me,
A truth hidden, a secret decree.
But time has passed, hearts have changed,
And I'm left wondering if it's too late to rearrange.

***

I wonder how fate can favour me,
Grant me a dashing person like you,
So modern and polished, not a boy but a powerful man,
I don't even know how to react, but then you say,

**

"All these years, I've never forgotten you,
You've always been the one I'd run to."

And with those words, my heart skips a beat,
For in this moment, destiny feels so sweet.

"Modern you and modern me, makes the perfect romance ever."

BRING A ROSE

***

   It was a beautiful morning, the sun's first light,
   Painting the sky in crimson bright.
   Gold and scarlet, a wondrous blend,
   A masterpiece that knows no end.

**

   The scent of roses filled the air,
   A fragrance is soft beyond compare.
   Fern leaves danced in the whispering breeze,
   Swaying gently with such ease.

**

   Each breath I took, so pure, so free,
   The wind played softly, embracing me.
   But in that moment, lost in time,
   Bittersweet memories filled my mind.

***

   I remember the olden days, free of regret,
   Each moment with him, I cannot forget.

A smile lingers, soft and genuine,
As memories dance in faded hue.

**

But my health wanes, fragile and frail,
A whispering wind, a fleeting tale.
I know my body won't last the night,
Soon wrapped in white, still and tight.

**

Dressed as the rich in garments pristine,
Yet no mourning eyes will be seen.
Unlike before, no tears will fall,
No grieving voices, no cries at all.

***

That morning, I held a mirror nearby,
A stranger's face began to appear.
The golden locks of yesterday's light
Had faded to silver, dull and slight.

**

Once playful curls, now straight and bare,
A silent whisper of time's affair.
My eyes, once bright with endless cheer,
Now traced with lines of passing years.

**

Crow's feet danced where laughter lay,
My nose now wrinkled in dismay.
My face, like paper, torn and creased,
An old love letter, long dismissed.

BRING A ROSE

***

Speaking of love letters, my hand took flight,
Penning words beneath the moon's soft light.
Dear Lost Lover, decades have passed,
Since our eyes met, since I saw you last.

**

Perhaps now, with time's cruel art,
A wheelchair holds your weary heart,
Or crutches guide your faltering stride,
Or boredom lingers at your side.

**

Yet, I recall our fleeting days,
Youthful whispers, sunlit haze.
Moments unspoken, tender, faithful,
But never did I confess to you.

**

How foolish was I to fear your scorn,
To silence a love so gently born?
Now, I wonder what held me back—
A ghost of doubt, a heart off track.

***

Somehow, we drifted like leaves in the breeze,
Choices led us down separate seas.
Fear, fate, and time, a cruel design,
Conspired to sever your heart from mine.

***

I wish I could meet you once more,

Just to see you, to touch you—nothing more.
One last time, a fleeting embrace,
To trace the love time can't be erased.

**

Did you have children, a life untold?
Grandchildren with laughter bright and bold?
I never could love another soul,
None, but you could make me whole.

**

Lovers came, mere passing flames,
Carnal whispers, forgotten names.
None could capture, none could stay,
Like you did, in love's way.

**

I roamed the world, sought gold and fame,
Treasures vast—but none your name.
And when my strength began to fade,
I lived where lifeless souls were laid.

**

No house, no hearth, no place to rest,
Only you felt at home, and it felt best.
My happy place, my shelter authentic,
There were never walls—only you.

***

I dreamed of you in dusk and dawn,
Hoping fate would lead you on.
But time was cruel, and it passed me by,
And never once met your eye.

**

Now sickness grips my fragile frame,
A whispered curse, a dying flame.
The wind it chills me to the bone,
I face the end, afraid, alone.

**

No longer fair, nor young, nor bright,
A fading ghost in the pale moonlight.
Yet, if your arms could hold me tight,
My soul would rest, and my heart would take flight.

***

If I could turn back the hands of time,
I'd whisper love in every rhyme.
I'd lay my heart unmasked, untrue,
And spill the words I owed to you.

**

Each day, I'd weave them soft and sweet,
A melody our souls would meet.
And in your arms, so safe, so warm,
I'd bloom like roses after a storm.

***

I have lost my way in time's embrace,
My fleeting steps will leave no trace.
The world moves on, yet here I lie,
Alone beneath the weeping sky.

**

By the time your eyes find these lines,
I'll rest where earth and silence bind.

A nameless stone, a fading name,
A whisper lost in fate's cruel game.

**

But if you ever seek my place,
Bring a rose with gentle grace.
You knew I loved them—perhaps you've forgot,
Yet grant me this, my final thought.

(Don't ever wait until it's too late.)

KISS YOU GOODBYE

***

The morning is misty, the fog drapes the land,
Blurring horizons, distant and grand.
I stand on the porch, silent and still,
As the cold breeze whispers, sharp with its chill.

**

I shiver; I sigh as the frost lingers near,
Wrapping my coat, drawing it near.
Yet through the grey, my heart still roves,
Longing for the sharp lines it loves.

***

As always, your face is so calm, so accurate,
Emerges softly in misty hues.
Solemn, beautiful, etched in my mind,
A love once near is now lost in time.

**

It should be you who warms me so,
Not this furred coat against the snow.

I always loved your warm embrace,
The gentle touch, the sacred place.

***

You'd warm me, your gaze so bright,
Eyes alight like morning's light.
You'd hold me close in tender grace,
Hands tracing love in a slow embrace.

**

From shoulders down to waist, so dear,
Your touch would chase away the chill and fear.
Softly murmuring words so sweet,
A love so whole, so pure, complete.

**

And in that glow, we'd steal the time,
Before the world reclaimed our minds.
Moments cherished, deep and true,
Before our work called me from you.

***

But those heart-warming moments fade,
When memory drifts to the night, you strayed.
The night you left, a shadow tall,
Your silhouette, my final call.

**

Your hair was tied as it always was,
Cornrows bouncing, locked in trust.
A Samsonian trunk in hands so strong,
While I stood frozen, lost, withdrawn.

**

A short note rested in my grasp,
Too small to hold the love that passed.
Tears fell hot, like burning rain,
Staining my skin with sorrow's pain.

***

Before you left, without a glance,
I never thought I'd lose my chance.
I never knew your love could wane,
That you could be the source of pain.

**

Strangely, I never ran to plead,
No desperate cries, no broken need.
Perhaps, I thought, I was unworthy,
A love misplaced, a heart unsteady.

**

Did I shame you? Did I fail?
Was I so weak, so frail, so pale?
I asked myself in days so long,
Wondering where I went so wrong.

***

Right now, I surrender to fate's gentle sway,
Trusting in time, come what may.
If we're meant to be, the stars will align,
If not, I'll treasure the moments you were mine.

**

I'll bask in the glow of love once shared,
When I felt cherished, deeply cared.

A warmth that lingers, soft and bright,
Guiding me gently through the night.

***

I always thought you were my fate,
My soulmate is true, my destined mate.
But I was wrong, and now I stand,
With shattered hearts and empty hands.

**

A thousand pieces, torn, unhealed,
Yet still, I wait—my love concealed.
If ever you call, if you return,
My arms stay open, and my heart still burns.

***

I always wonder, night and day,
Why did you leave without a say?
Why you didn't let me kiss you goodbye,
A final touch before goodbye.

**

Had your lips met mine once more,
Their warmth would linger at my core.
A trace of you, a soulful thread,
To hold onto while tears were shed.

**

But now I wait, with lips so bare,
Longing for a love once there.
Hoping still, through time and pain,
That you might find your way again.

KISS YOU GOODBYE

(Never be without hope, in the end all shall be well)

FRIENDSHIP

***

Friendship is that thing,
That's patched together,
By compassion, commitment,
Patience and love forever.

**

It's the bond that grows,
Through highs and lows,
A connection deep and true,
That sees us through and through.

***

And you, my friend, don't let go of my hand,
Lock up my secrets deep inside your soul,
Let's be each other's light in the darkness of the world,
And rejoice together on the bright day, whole.

**

In every storm, we'll stand side by side,
With unwavering hearts, we'll take this ride.

Through every trial, we'll find our way,
And bask in the joy of a brighter day.

***

Don't hide your flaws from me,
Let's be open and honest,
God be our witness,
As we swear this oath, and He helps us never stray,
From this bond, through all our lifetimes.

**

In truth, we stand firm, hand in hand,
Through every trial, we'll understand.
With love and trust as our guide,
Together, we'll walk with hearts open wide.

***

For now, let us keep on dreaming,
Texting and calling, wishing each other well,
When we are old, and our hair is grey,
These memories will warm us like a gentle spell.

**

In the quiet moments, we'll reminisce,
Of days filled with laughter, love, and bliss.
And though time may pass and seasons change,
Our hearts will stay forever, never estranged.

(I'm not God to know tomorrow, but little I have we will share)

III

LOVE, LIFE AND LIES

YOUR LOVE REMINDS ME...

***

Your love reminds me of a well so deep,
A timeless flow, a promise to keep.
Never dry, never gone,
Endless as the breaking dawn.

**

Like a hill dressed in evergreen,
Steady, pure, forever seen.
Like summer skies where bright suns burn,
A warmth to which my heart returns.

**

Like a night so soft, so wide,
With a graceful moon in silver pride.
Gloried by a million stars above,
Shining proper—just like our love.

***

All those are beautiful, magical, and true,
Just like the love I found in you.

Unconditional, pure, a gift so rare,
A love that lingers in the air.

**

For all you've given, I can't repay,
No words could ever honestly say.
But know this much: through joy and pain,
I'd trust you with my heart again.

(Love runs deeper than looks, always love people for who they are; their hearts, body and soul no matter how flawed they might be)

I DON'T REMEMBER WHEN...

***

I don't recall a time before this,
Feeling wanted, needed—wrapped in bliss.
Loved so deeply, wild and free,
A love so vast, it swallows me.

**

My heart is heavy, yet light as air,
With feelings new, so pure, so rare.
Sweet as honey, soft as a sigh,
You are the one who makes me fly.

**

I feel your love deep in my soul,
Your whispers make my heartbeat roll.
I've placed my heart in your hands,
To cherish, to break—by fate's demands.

**

Yet come what may, through time untold,
You'll have a space within my soul.

First Creation

For first love never fades away,
It lingers, even when hearts stray.

(People who thinks love is not enough, they haven't found their own true love)

SLAP OF REALITY

***

Whenever you feel like you're on cloud nine,
Reality swoops in to draw the line.
A slap, a jolt, to bring you down,
But lessons hide in every frown.

**

Don't live on mayhap, don't dwell on fate,
Mistakes we make, but they don't define our state.
Without misfortunes, miracles wouldn't shine,
Every fall leads to a rise, a climb.

**

Everything happens for a reason, you'll see,
In each twist of life, there's a key.
Own your actions, the paths you take,
Growth comes with each mistake.

***

For every day, karma writes its script,
A drama unfolds with every twist.

No matter what, don't sell your worth,
Or risk losing yourself for what it's worth.

**

You might find yourself lost and small,
A pawn in the game with no control at all.
But that's life's truth, as time goes by—
A dance of choices beneath the sky.

(Speak your truth before you are lied to)

THE MONSTER

***
We used to be so mad in love,
We don't see eye to eye; it's hard to rise above.
In truth, I'll try not to let tears fall,
Instead, I'll fly away, far from it all.

**
I'll forget the tender love we shared,
The breakfast tray, the kisses you dared.
Whispering sweet words in the quiet of the morn,
Now, it just echoes, with hearts torn.

***
For all those moments vanished like dreams,
Along with our love, torn at the seams.
You led me deep into the dark,
Sucking the light, leaving no spark.

**
A broken heart, a soul bruised deep,
I'm left to gather what's left to keep.

First Creation

The light you took, the love you stole,
Now, I stand with an empty soul.

***

I hope wherever you are,
You lie still, watching from afar.
Prepared to face the monster you've made,
Born of hatred, in shadows, it's laid.

**

A creature born of malice deep,
Now, stalking the silence where you sleep.
The echoes of pain you once fed,
Return to haunt you, where you tread.

(Some things are lost in life so that we can find others, maybe not as great as what was lost but a great deal more satisfying)

SAVE ME

***

Ever felt lonely in a crowd,
That's a cliché we all know too well,
Ever felt virtual but living in real life?
I am not sure how to say this,
Because what I am feeling maybe doesn't have a name.

**

It's like being here but not quite *here*,
A ghost in the moment, caught in a sphere.
I reach out, but the world feels too far,
And wonder if this emptiness is just who we are.

***

Calling it depression,
I would be casting myself to doomsday,
Calling it loneliness,
Well, that's an understatement,
Not of the year, of the millennia.

**

It's a quiet ache, a weight without a name,
An endless dance of a flickering flame.
A place where no one can quite see,
The quiet storm raged inside me.

***

Can I cry?
That's dumb,
Cause there are millions,
Of unsheltered people, desperate,
And know how bitter life can be.

**

But in the silence, I find my tears,
Falling for those who've lived through fears.
Yet, even in my struggle, I see,
That pain is something we all set free.

***

Every story of tragedy
Has its uniqueness,
Which makes you feel crumbly and heartbroken.
You get the idea, right?

**

Then after, you feel like shit,
Numb all over, unable to fit.
The weight of it all just drags you down,
And you wonder if you'll ever turn it around.

***

As for myself,
Trust me, I do work,

And I try to find the meaning of my life,
Still, fate seems to be like
Playing peekaboo with me.

**

I reach, I search, I strive to grow,
But every step feels like a shadow,
Just when I think I'm on the right track,
Fate pulls me back, leaving me to crack.

***

I feel good in the shadow of death,
In my sleep,
Slumber pulls me in,
Holds me close,
Real-life fades away, and then dreams soothe me.

**

In that quiet place, I'm free,
Where the weight of the world can't reach me.
The silence wraps me like a tender hug,
And in that stillness, I feel love.

***

My daydreams and fantasies
Have become the lifeless, bleak stones,
I no longer find an escape there.
Conjuring good things was my regular habit,
But even now, that has become so boring.

**

What once sparked joy now feels flat,
It's like a tired story with no ending.

The colours fade, the visions blur,
And I'm left wondering where I once were.

***

Songs and beautiful paintings,
Good movies and funny comedies,
Watching them, to me, feels like a chore,
That is what I have to do in this modern world.
Except that sometimes, I hide behind words, I write.

**

The colours fade, the laughter dulls,
A world of noise, where silence pulls.
But in the quiet, with pen in hand,
I find a space where I can stand.

***

Shall I wait for the apocalypse?
To come and wipe off humankind,
On the other hand, shall I expect some alien invasion?
That will dominate the world.
Either way, death would maybe suit me fine.
My soul cries.

**

In the darkness, I find no light,
Only endless shadows, devoid of sight.
The weight of it all too much to bear,
I wonder if anyone out there even cares.

***

My heart bleeds,
My body endures,

SAVE ME

Nevertheless, I am hurting; I am setting an SOS.
See me, hear me, and save me.
I beg.

**

In this silent cry, I search for a hand,
A lifeline, a way to understand.
Through the pain, through the tears, I fight,

Hoping someone will bring me light.

LOST AND NEVER FOUND

***

There was this time in my life,
I wanted things that I could not afford,
I craved things that were beyond my reach,
I fancied people that would never look at me twice,
And I didn't understand myself.

**

In the silence of my desires, I wandered,
Chasing shadows of dreams, I pondered.
Lost in the wanting, I forgot to see,
That what I needed was already inside me.

***

That was a moment where everything was just dreams,
All were just fantasies that would maybe never happen.
I was just my shadow, and me,
Nobody would even care because
They may have thought I was a psychopath.

**

In the stillness, I faded unseen,
Caught between what was and could have been.
I wore my pain like a hidden crown,
Hoping someone would look and pull me down.

***

I saw them bloom,
Their laughter was like petals unfolding,
Their dreams soaring, untamed,
While I stood still—unchanged, unseen,
Not poor, not rich, just average.

**

Not super ugly or classically beautiful, only plain,
Not a genius, nor outright dumb, only dull.
A spectator in a world that kept spinning,
Watching nature grow and glow,
People alike, while I remained… just me.

***

But inside of me was this voice
Of hope and belief
That said, I should not give up
Even if I have not figured it out
One day it will be alright.

***

I held on to that voice
When the situation worsened,
My faith grew stronger,
And my hope withheld me together,
And I stood in the world unnoticed, not that I didn't want to be.

***

Every day and every hour
Some kind of a guardian angel
Stood by me, murmuring kind words
Relief and bliss would wash over me
And I would listen closely as she said.

***

"Look up in my eyes
Listen to my words, lean into my touch
As I reach to your soul
I will heal your wounds
Mend where you were broken."

***

A soul adrift in the winds of time,
Hoping for light, yet embracing the dim,
Each day, a whisper, a silent rhyme,
Waiting for fate to call upon him.

**

Nothing happened, yet everything passed,
Dreams unshaken but never profound,
A journey of hope, though never steadfast,
In the end, I was lost, never found.

(Life will not always be what you hope for or predict, but when your faith is strong, fears writhe away, you spend your days happy and content, until you die)

INFINITE LOOP

***

   Our lives are strange
   Stranger than we care to admit,
   Looking closer,
   What seemed small will look gigantic
   And what seemed weak will be strong.

***

   The universe itself
   Holds a million stories,
   The planets and the void space
   Then the stars and black holes
   And all of these are in a forever motion.

***

   Take the earth, for instance,
   Where we live
   With more than a million of other living things,
   Humans are the major ones,
   And the most complicated ones.

***

Humans for over the years,
They leave their promises unfulfilled
Like the flowers that bloom then wither
Humans backstab each other
Like the mountains, which are strong but later weather,

***

Time and again,
Humans might look acquiescent
Yet they're tumultuous inside.
Lies and truths
Are all mixed up, not at all like paraffin and water.

***

All these things
The birth and deaths
The interactions,
The contradictions,
Have gone on and on.

***

But nobody and not anything
Has been able to stop these
Nobody is clear about his or her existence
It's a string of never-ending arguments
And the universe stays in that infinite loop.

(Moreover, I see myself, as a rose, simple and single, singing songs of sadness and despair, yet hoping to soar high one day, beyond the skies, and real life, will that happen? Selah.)

***

What's possible now?
Is to calm my soul
I feel myself roaming in the universe
Let it consume me completely,
Be one with that infinite loop.

(Of all magic and powers, please grant me invisibility)

IV

PASSION AND SELF-LOVE

ANOTHER HEART

***

Is there another heart out there,
That beats like mine, so pure, so bare?
One that feels as deep as the sea,
And opens up, unafraid, to me?

**

A soul that warms with tender grace,
That sees my dreams and takes their place.
To understand, to honestly know,
To walk beside me, let love grow.

***

Please tell me there's another heart,
That loves with no conditions to impart.
A soul that gives with joy so true,
Caring with no reason, just pure and new.

**

One that sees the good in me,
Yet accepts my flaws wholeheartedly.

Not seeking perfection, nor asking why,
Just holding me close as time drifts by.

***

If yours is another heart so true,
That loves the words, the sky's soft hue,
That cherishes people, nature's grace,
And finds in peace a sacred place—

**

Then come, take my hand, let's flee,
To where the soul roams wild and free.
Where love is pure, and hearts can grow,
If you are ready—then let's go.

***

Let's soar high without a limit,
Beyond the norm, beyond the timid.
Come closer, fear not my touch,
I promise I won't ask too much.

**

Join me if your heart beats free,
If love and dreams are meant to be.
Leap, don't turn away,
Let's chase the light, come what may.

(Sometimes, the ties of the heart are stronger than those of blood)

FOUNTAIN OF ECSTASY

***

Soldiers find their pride in the fight,
Inspired by honour, by land's pure light.
With every plan, each move well made,
They march forward, unafraid.

**

Victory earned, they stand so tall,
Celebrating triumph, answering the call.
Yet on watch still, ever aware,
Guarding their land with hearts laid bare.

***

Singers find their joy, their bliss,
In beats that pulse, in rhythms that twist.
Smooth voices soaring, wild raps that flow,
They light up the stage, putting on a show.

**

Crowds in a frenzy lost in the sound,
Their hearts beat faster, all around.

A moment of magic, a shared delight,
In the music, they find their light.

***

Writers, they create, and they kill,
Breathing life, then silence still.
They weave miracles from their mind,
A tapestry of the soul they find.

**

Sometimes, it's love, a sweet embrace,
Other times, sorrow leaves its trace.
Cutting deep, through heart and bone,
In their words, emotions are sown.

***

Then poets, the lovers of words,
Dig deeper, where silence is heard.
To the core of all, they seek and find,
Unveiling truths that stir the mind.

**

They release words of praise, pure and bright,
Or cast shadows with slander's bite.
Through verses, they shape the world anew,
In their lines, the old and the true.

***

It seems like sweet words emanate from their souls,
Flowing like rivers, making hearts whole.
They see the world magnified, aglow,
Understanding ecstasy in places below.

**

    The fountains of joy, so deep, so pure,
    Buried in the earth's quiet allure.
    The same Earth that once was bare,
    Until God's grace brought life to share.

**

    With humans, he filled the void, the night,
    Turning barren lands into a world of light.
    A canvas for dreams, for love, for pain,
    In our hands, his creation remains.

FALL IN LOVE WITH POETRY

***

Soul pours words,
Mind leaking
Fingers typing
On a hyper-speed
I'm turning sore, yet I don't take a break.

***

My head pounds
My heart clamours against my chest
Passion burns me,
I scribble down my fantasy
And lay it down for the world to see.

***

I don't care if they laugh.
I am working up the ladder,
Poetry is a part of me,
And I don't seek fame,
Alternatively, even glory.

***

All I want is the grace,
To drip from my stances,
On glance at the lines
You fall in love
With poetry, forever.

POET IN A WARRIOR

***

She is one of a kind,
The type of a woman you won't find anywhere,
The different one
For she smiles,
Just at the beauty of the earth.

***

She's a kindred spirit,
Who overlooks the worst?
To find the little good qualities,
And sweetness in the world,
To relish in.

***

She was hurt,
But she laughs
She was betrayed,
But she trusts
Once left alone, she still loves.

***

She's not some disillusioned gir.l
But mature and realistic
She's a fighter but has a heart of a poet,
She keeps her faith strong to shield her
From the bitterness of the world.

***

See things from her angle.
You'll pray to live a hundred more years
For she is just a humble lover of nature,
But a fierce fighter,
She is the poet in a warrior.

> (Ladies, we would all want to be like this, and we can make it happen; gents, never settle for a woman less than this)

FIRST CREATION

***

Everything in the world
It is infinite to us.
A person can never know.
What exactly has happened?
What will happen, or even what is happening now?

***

Inside myself,
I feel a burning passion
A force pushing me
There is a light,
That I know will lead me through the dark.

***

I am on a journey,
A real long one
I am in a battle
That I have won
But I have to prove my victory repeatedly.

FIRST CREATION

***

This is my first creation,
A small chunk
Of the thoughts
And emotions in me,
For day by day, mysteries are woven into my soul's depths.

(Poetry is not about the dainty, classic, Shakespearian English but about the feelings from the depths of our hearts.)

Epilogue

Every poem in this collection is a fragment of a soul—my soul, your soul, and the soul of those who have loved, lost, fought, and hoped. Words may fade, but their emotions will always remain, woven into the hearts of those who dare to feel.

From the echoes of Africa's past to the whispers of love and heartbreak, from the shadows of doubt to the light of self-discovery, this journey has been more than ink on pages—it has been a testimony of resilience, identity and the eternal search for meaning.

Poetry is not merely written; it is lived. It breathes through the ones who embrace its rhythm, find comfort in its embrace, and let it speak when silence weighs too heavy.

If you have felt something—joy, sorrow, nostalgia, or hope—then this creation has fulfilled its purpose. Let these words stay with you, grow within you, and when you need them most, may they find you again.

Every ending is but a new beginning.

Afterword

This poetry collection serves as a heartfelt reflection of my innermost thoughts and stirring emotions, encapsulating a profound piece of my journey woven into words. I pour out the essence of my experiences with each line, showcasing the beauty and pain alike. Even as I write this, I am acutely aware that an ocean of feelings remains yet to be explored and expressed. This collection, however, represents my inaugural stride into the enchanting realm of poetry—a tender beginning filled with hope and vulnerability as I invite you to join me on this journey of discovery.

As a young writer, I am on a profound journey, navigating the intricate tapestry of life and its myriad aspects. With each word I pen, I weave my dreams and fears together, revealing my innermost thoughts to the world. Although my experience is limited, my passion burns brightly, illuminating the path ahead. I tread this unpredictable sea of creativity, embracing the exhilarating highs and sobering lows accompanying my exploration. Each moment is a dance with uncertainty, a blend of joy and trepidation, as I immerse myself in storytelling, eager to share my evolving voice with an audience just beginning to discover the depths of my soul.

I genuinely hope you discover moments of joy and inspiration within these pages, just as I have found profound happiness in writing each word. It's interesting to note that every time I revisit this collection, I find myself engulfed in a wave of self-doubt, a gentle reminder that I, too, need to heed my advice. It's a strange and bittersweet feeling to stand as a beacon of encouragement for others while yearning for that same light to guide me through my moments of uncertainty and hesitation.

Immerse yourself in the pages before you, letting the words wash over you like a gentle wave. As you delve into each poem, remember that I, too, am on this journey where I pour every emotion, every fragment of my soul, onto the page. With each line I write, I strive to grow as a poet and a human being, exploring the depths of this beautiful craft, one heartfelt poem at a time. Together, let's embrace the magic of expression and the power of vulnerability.

Sandra Nadege

About the Author

Sandra Nadege is a poet and author who was born and raised in Kigali, Rwanda. She enjoys writing almost everything, from poems to articles and short stories to novels. Her works have appeared in anthologies like 60 Seconds of Silence. First Creation is her first published collection of poetry. She is a member of many writing and reading groups. Meanwhile, she enjoys reading poems, thrillers, and romances as she works on more books of her own.

www.ingramcontent.com/pod-product-compliance
Lightning Source LLC
LaVergne TN
LVHW010602070526
838199LV00063BA/5043